LEARNING SPANISH FOR SCHOOL STUDENTS

DR DHEERAJ MEHROTRA

Copyright © Dr Dheeraj Mehrotra
All Rights Reserved.

This book has been self-published with all reasonable efforts taken to make the material error-free by the author. No part of this book shall be used, reproduced in any manner whatsoever without written permission from the author, except in the case of brief quotations embodied in critical articles and reviews.

The Author of this book is solely responsible and liable for its content including but not limited to the views, representations, descriptions, statements, information, opinions and references ["Content"]. The Content of this book shall not constitute or be construed or deemed to reflect the opinion or expression of the Publisher or Editor. Neither the Publisher nor Editor endorse or approve the Content of this book or guarantee the reliability, accuracy or completeness of the Content published herein and do not make any representations or warranties of any kind, express or implied, including but not limited to the implied warranties of merchantability, fitness for a particular purpose. The Publisher and Editor shall not be liable whatsoever for any errors, omissions, whether such errors or omissions result from negligence, accident, or any other cause or claims for loss or damages of any kind, including without limitation, indirect or consequential loss or damage arising out of use, inability to use, or about the reliability, accuracy or sufficiency of the information contained in this book.

Made with ♥ on the Notion Press Platform
www.notionpress.com

Contents

Preface

Language empowers exposure to different cultures, ideas, and possibilities. Spanish, one of the most commonly spoken languages, connects millions worldwide. In today's interconnected world, learning Spanish is essential for academic advancement, travel, and personal enrichment.

Learning Spanish for School Students is an organised, engaging, and practical guide to teaching young learners Spanish. The content is designed for schoolchildren, making learning easy and fun. Each chapter covers basic vocabulary, grammar, and phrases with exercises and real-world examples.

We use dialogues, cultural insights, and entertaining activities to make language learning fun and natural. From greetings and regular discussions to complex topics, this book gives students confidence in Spanish communication.

Learning a new language involves appreciating its culture. We build a greater understanding of global diversity as we teach kids about Spanish-speaking countries' unique cultures, customs, and history.

We think language learning should be fun and educational. Students should practise often, immerse themselves in Spanish-speaking situations, and, most importantly, have fun learning!

Author

ONE
ALPHABETS OF SPANISH LANGUAGE

The Spanish alphabet has 27 letters (including ñ).

Here they are with their pronunciations:

Letter - Pronunciation

A/a/ (ah)

B/be/ (beh)

C/θe/ or /se/ (theh or seh)

D/de/ (deh)

E/e/ (eh)

F/efe/ (eh-feh)

G/xe/ (heh)

H/a ʧe/ (ah-cheh)

I/i/ (ee)

J/xota/ (ho-tah)

K/ka/ (kah)

L/ele/ (eh-leh)

M/eme/ (eh-meh)

N/ene/ (eh-neh)

Ñ/eɲe/ (eh-nyeh)

O/o/ (oh)

P/pe/ (peh)

Q/ku/ (koo)

R/ere/ (eh-reh)

S/ese/ (eh-seh)

T/te/ (teh)

U/u/ (oo)

V/uve/ (oo-veh)

W/doble uve/ (doh-bleh oo-veh)

X/ekis/ (eh-kees)

Y/i griega/ (ee gree-eh-gah)

Z/θeta/ or /seta/ (theh-tah or seh-tah)

Key Differences:

Ñ: Spanish has an additional letter, ñ (eñe), which is pronounced like "ny" in "canyon."

Pronunciation:

Spanish letters are generally pronounced more consistently than English letters.

Double Letters:

In Spanish, ch, ll, and rr were once considered separate letters but are now treated as digraphs (combinations of two letters).

Spanish Alphabet Multiple-Choice Questions

1. How many letters are there in the Spanish alphabet?
   A) 26
B) 27
C) 28
D) 29
Answer: B) 27
   2. Which of the following is an additional letter in the Spanish alphabet that does not exist in the English alphabet?
   A) LL
B) RR
C) Ñ
D) CH

Answer: C) Ñ

    3. How is the letter "A" pronounced in Spanish?

    A) Ay

B) Ah

C) Uh

D) Aw

Answer: B) Ah

    4. What is the correct pronunciation of the letter "C" in Spanish before "E" or "I" (in Spain)?

    A) Seh

B) Theh

C) Cheh

D) Keh

Answer: B) Theh

    5. How is the letter "G" pronounced before "E" or "I" in Spanish?

    A) Heh

B) Geh

C) Keh

D) Seh

Answer: A) Heh

    6. What is the name of the letter "H" in Spanish?

    A) Hota

B) Aʧe

C) Efe

D) I griega

Answer: B) Aʧe

    7. How is "J" pronounced in Spanish?

    A) Yeh

B) Ho-tah

C) Kah

D) Seh

Answer: B) Ho-tah

    8. What is the correct pronunciation of the letter "E" in Spanish?

    A) Ee

B) Eh

C) Ay

D) Uh

Answer: B) Eh

9. How is the letter "Q" pronounced in Spanish?

A) Koo

B) Keh

C) Kue

D) Kah

Answer: A) Koo

10. What is the correct pronunciation of "Ñ"?

A) En-yeh

B) Eh-neh

C) Eh-leh

D) Ee-nyeh

Answer: A) En-yeh

11. How is "U" pronounced in Spanish?

A) Uh

B) Oo

C) Ah

D) Ow

Answer: B) Oo

12. What is the correct pronunciation of the letter "V" in Spanish?

A) Veh

B) Beh

C) Oo-veh

D) Doble veh

Answer: C) Oo-veh

13. What is the pronunciation of "X" in Spanish?

A) Eh-kees

B) Seh

C) Koo

D) Heh

Answer: A) Eh-kees

14. What is another name for the letter "Y" in Spanish?

A) I latina

B) I griega

C) Jota

D) Eh-yeh

Answer: B) I griega

15. Which of these letter combinations were previously considered separate letters in Spanish?

A) Ch, Ll, Rr

B) Sh, Th, Ch

C) Ll, X, Z

D) Ch, Gh, Ñ

Answer: A) Ch, Ll, Rr

16. How is "Z" pronounced in Spain?

A) Theh-tah

B) Seh-tah

C) Cheh-tah

D) Zeh-tah

Answer: A) Theh-tah

17. How do you pronounce "B" in Spanish?

A) Be

B) Beh

C) Boo

D) Breh

Answer: B) Beh

18. What is the pronunciation of "F" in Spanish?

A) Eff

B) Feh

C) Efe

D) Eh-feh

Answer: D) Eh-feh

19. How is "D" pronounced in Spanish?

A) Deh

B) Doh

C) Duh

D) Dah

Answer: A) Deh

20. Which letter in Spanish is always silent?

A) J

B) H

C) Ñ

D) G

Answer: B) H

21. What is the full pronunciation of "W" in Spanish?

A) Doble uve

B) Doble ve

C) Doble u

D) Uve doble

Answer: A) Doble uve

22. What is the pronunciation of "L" in Spanish?

A) Ele

B) El-leh

C) Eñe

D) Eh-yeh

Answer: A) Ele

23. Which of the following is NOT a letter in the Spanish alphabet?

A) Ñ

B) CH

C) LL

D) SH

Answer: D) SH

24. How is "R" pronounced in Spanish?

A) Er-reh

B) Eh-reh

C) Ruh

D) Eh-yeh

Answer: B) Eh-reh

25. How many vowel letters are there in the Spanish alphabet?

A) 4

B) 5

C) 6

D) 7

Answer: B) 5

❧❧❧

TWO
SPANISH NUMBERS

Basic Numbers

Here are the basic numbers from 0 to 10 in Spanish:

| Number | Spanish | Pronunciation |

|--------|----------|-----------------|

| 0 | cero | SEH-roh |

| 1 | uno | OO-noh |

| 2 | dos | DOHS |

| 3 | tres | TREHS |

| 4 | cuatro | KWAH-troh |

| 5 | cinco | SEEN-koh |

| 6 | seis | SAYS |

| 7 | siete | SYEH-teh |

| 8 | ocho | OH-choh |

| 9 | nueve | NWEH-beh |

| 10 | diez | DYEHS |

Numbers 11 to 20

The numbers from 11 to 20 have unique names:

| Number | Spanish | Pronunciation |

|--------|-----------|------------------|

| 11 | once | OHN-seh |

| 12 | doce | DOH-seh |

| 13 | trece | TREH-seh |

| 14 | catorce | kah-TOR-seh |

| 15 | quince | KEEN-seh |

| 16 | dieciséis | dee-eh-see-SAYS |

| 17 | diecisiete| dee-eh-see-EH-teh |

| 18 | dieciocho | dee-eh-see-OH-cho |

| 19 | diecinueve| dee-eh-see-NWEH-beh |

| 20 | veinte | BAIN-teh |

Tens and Beyond

After 20, the numbers follow a pattern. Here are the tens:

| Number | Spanish | Pronunciation |

|--------|-----------|------------------|

| 30 | treinta | TREHN-tah |

| 40 | cuarenta | kwah-REN-tah |

| 50 | cincuenta | seen-KWEN-tah |

| 60 | sesenta | seh-SEN-tah |

| 70 | setenta | seh-TEN-tah |

| 80 | ochenta | oh-CHEN-tah |

| 90 | noventa | noh-VEN-tah |

| 100 | cien | SYEN |

Forming Numbers

To form numbers between the tens, you combine the tens with the units. For example:

21 = veintiuno (veinte + uno)

35 = treinta y cinco (treinta + y + cinco)

47 = cuarenta y siete (cuarenta + y + siete)

Hundreds and Thousands

100 = cien (for exactly 100) or ciento (for numbers between 101-199)

200 = doscientos

300 = trescientos

400 = cuatrocientos

500 = quinientos

600 = seiscientos

700 = setecientos

800 = ochocientos

900 = novecientos

1000 = mil

Spanish Numbers Multiple-Choice Questions

1. What is the Spanish word for 0?
    A) Cero
B) Uno
C) Cien
D) Mil
Answer: A) Cero
    2. How do you say "5" in Spanish?
    A) Tres
B) Cuatro
C) Cinco
D) Seis
Answer: C) Cinco
    3. What is the pronunciation of "8" in Spanish?
    A) OH-choh
B) OCH-en-tah

C) OCH-oh

D) OH-chay

Answer: A) OH-choh

4. What is the correct Spanish number for "12"?

A) Once

B) Doce

C) Trece

D) Quince

Answer: B) Doce

5. How do you say "14" in Spanish?

A) Cuatro

B) Catorce

C) Quince

D) Dieciseis

Answer: B) Catorce

6. What is the Spanish word for "17"?

A) Dieciséis

B) Diecisiete

C) Dieciocho

D) Diecinueve

Answer: B) Diecisiete

7. How do you say "20" in Spanish?

A) Veinte

B) Veintiuno

C) Cien

D) Treinta

Answer: A) Veinte

8. What is the Spanish word for "30"?

A) Treinta

B) Trece

C) Cuarenta

D) Quince

Answer: A) Treinta

9. What is the correct pronunciation of "40" in Spanish?

A) kwah-REN-tah

B) kwah-TREN-tah

C) keh-REN-tah

D) kwah-REH-tah

Answer: A) kwah-REN-tah

10. How do you say "50" in Spanish?

A) Sesenta

B) Cincuenta

C) Setenta

D) Ochenta

Answer: B) Cincuenta

11. What is the Spanish number for "60"?

A) Setenta

B) Cincuenta

C) Sesenta

D) Ochenta

Answer: C) Sesenta

12. How do you say "80" in Spanish?

A) Noventa

B) Ochenta

C) Cuarenta

D) Setenta

Answer: B) Ochenta

13. What is the Spanish word for "100"?

A) Ciento

B) Mil

C) Cien

D) Quinientos

Answer: C) Cien

14. How do you say "101" in Spanish?

A) Cien uno

B) Ciento uno

C) Mil uno

D) Cien diez

Answer: B) Ciento uno

15. How do you say "200" in Spanish?

A) Doscientos

B) Doscientas

C) Doscient

D) Cien dos

Answer: A) Doscientos

16. What is the Spanish number for "400"?

A) Cuatrocientos

B) Cuatrocientos diez

C) Cuatrocienta

D) Cuatromil

Answer: A) Cuatrocientos

17. How do you say "500" in Spanish?

A) Cincocientos

B) Quinientos

C) Quincientos

D) Quinentos

Answer: B) Quinientos

18. What is the correct spelling of "600" in Spanish?

A) Seisciento

B) Seiscientos

C) Seiscentos

D) Seisientos

Answer: B) Seiscientos

19. How do you say "700" in Spanish?

A) Setecientos

B) Setenta

C) Sietecientos

D) Setencientos

Answer: A) Setecientos

20. What is the Spanish number for "900"?

A) Novecientos

B) Novecientas

C) Nueve cientos

D) Noventa y cien

Answer: A) Novecientos

21. How do you say "1000" in Spanish?

A) Mil

B) Cien

C) Mil uno

D) Mil ciento

Answer: A) Mil

22. How do you write "21" in Spanish?

A) Veintiuno

B) Veinte y uno

C) Veintuno

D) Ventiuno

Answer: A) Veintiuno

23. How do you say "35" in Spanish?

A) Treinta y cinco

B) Treinticinco

C) Treinta cinco

D) Trescincuenta

Answer: A) Treinta y cinco

24. How do you say "47" in Spanish?

A) Cuarenta siete

B) Cuarenta y siete

C) Cuarentisiete

D) Cuatrosetenta

Answer: B) Cuarenta y siete

25. What is "99" in Spanish?

A) Noventa nueve

B) Noventa y nueve

C) Noventinueve

D) Noventa nueve y

Answer: B) Noventa y nueve

𐤃𐤃𐤃

THREE
ASKING FOR DIRECTIONS

Basic Phrases to Ask for Directions

¿Dónde está...? - Where is...?

Example: ¿Dónde está el baño? (Where is the bathroom?)

¿Cómo llego a...? - How do I get to...?

Example: ¿Cómo llego a la estación de tren? (How do I get to the train station?)

¿Está lejos? - Is it far?

¿Está cerca? - Is it nearby?

¿Puede ayudarme? - Can you help me?

¿Hay un/una... por aquí? - Is there a... around here?

Example: ¿Hay un restaurante por aquí? (Is there a restaurant around here?)

¿Por dónde se va a...? - Which way do I go to...?

Example: ¿Por dónde se va al centro? (Which way do I go to the city center?)

Key Vocabulary for Directions

la calle - the street

la avenida - the avenue

la plaza - the square

el semáforo - the traffic light

la esquina - the corner

la derecha - the right

la izquierda - the left

todo recto - straight ahead

al final de - at the end of

cerca de - near

lejos de - far from

al lado de - next to

enfrente de - in front of

detrás de - behind

entre - between

Common Responses You Might Hear

Siga todo recto. - Go straight ahead.

Gire a la derecha. - Turn right.

Gire a la izquierda. - Turn left.

Está a la vuelta de la esquina. - It's around the corner.

Está a dos cuadras. - It's two blocks away.

Cruza la calle. - Cross the street.

Está al final de la calle. - It's at the end of the street.

Está cerca/lejos. - It's close/far.

Pase el semáforo. - Go past the traffic light.

No sé, lo siento. - I don't know, sorry.

Example Conversations

1. Asking for a Restaurant

You: Hola, ¿hay un restaurante por aquí?
(Hi, is there a restaurant around here?)

Local: Sí, hay uno a dos cuadras. Siga todo recto y gire a la izquierda en el semáforo.
(Yes, there's one two blocks away. Go straight and turn left at the traffic light.)

You: Muchas gracias.
(Thank you very much.)

2. Asking for the Train Station

You: Disculpe, ¿dónde está la estación de tren?
(Excuse me, where is the train station?)

Local: Está cerca. Camine todo recto y gire a la derecha en la plaza.
(It's close. Walk straight and turn right at the square.)

You: ¿Está lejos?
(Is it far?)

Local: No, está a cinco minutos.
(No, it's five minutes away.)

3. Asking for the Bathroom

You: ¿Dónde está el baño?
(Where is the bathroom?)

Local: Está al final del pasillo, a la izquierda.
(It's at the end of the hallway, on the left.)

You: Gracias.
(Thank you.)

Tips for Asking for Directions

Be polite: Start with "Disculpe" (Excuse me) or "Hola" (Hello).

Use gestures: Pointing or mimicking turns can help if you struggle with the language.

Repeat back: Confirm what you heard by repeating the directions.

Example: ¿Entonces, todo recto y luego a la derecha? (So, straight ahead and then to the right?)

Learn numbers: Knowing numbers will help you understand distances (e.g., dos cuadras - two blocks).

Spanish Directions Multiple-Choice Questions

1. How do you ask "Where is...?" in Spanish?

    A) ¿Cómo está...?

B) ¿Dónde está...?

C) ¿Qué es...?

D) ¿Cuándo está...?

Answer: B) ¿Dónde está...?

    2. What does "¿Cómo llego a...?" mean?

    A) Where is...?

B) How do I get to...?

C) Is it far?

D) Can I help you?

Answer: B) How do I get to...?

    3. How do you ask "Is it far?" in Spanish?

    A) ¿Está cerca?

B) ¿Está a la vuelta?

C) ¿Está lejos?

D) ¿Es lejos?

Answer: C) ¿Está lejos?

    4. What is the Spanish word for "street"?

    A) La esquina

B) La calle

C) La plaza

D) La avenida

Answer: B) La calle

    5. If someone says "Siga todo recto," what should you do?

    A) Turn left

B) Go straight ahead

C) Turn right

D) Cross the street

Answer: B) Go straight ahead

6. How do you say "Turn right" in Spanish?

A) Gire a la izquierda

B) Gire a la derecha

C) Todo recto

D) Cruza la calle

Answer: B) Gire a la derecha

7. What does "Está a la vuelta de la esquina" mean?

A) It's around the corner

B) It's on the left

C) It's two blocks away

D) It's in front of you

Answer: A) It's around the corner

8. What is the Spanish word for "traffic light"?

A) La plaza

B) El semáforo

C) La avenida

D) La calle

Answer: B) El semáforo

9. If you hear "Está cerca," what does it mean?

A) It's far

B) It's close

C) It's next to you

D) It's behind

Answer: B) It's close

10. How do you say "Cross the street" in Spanish?

A) Gire a la derecha

B) Cruza la calle

C) Está al final de la calle

D) Pase el semáforo

Answer: B) Cruza la calle

11. How do you ask "Can you help me?" in Spanish?

A) ¿Puedo ayudarle?

B) ¿Puede ayudarme?

C) ¿Cómo está usted?

D) ¿Dónde está?

Answer: B) ¿Puede ayudarme?

12. What does "entre" mean?

A) Behind

B) In front of

C) Between

D) Next to

Answer: C) Between

13. What is "next to" in Spanish?

A) Enfrente de

B) Al lado de

C) Detrás de

D) Lejos de

Answer: B) Al lado de

14. How do you say "at the end of" in Spanish?

A) Enfrente de

B) Detrás de

C) Al final de

D) Cerca de

Answer: C) Al final de

15. What is the Spanish phrase for "It's two blocks away"?

A) Está lejos de aquí

B) Está a dos cuadras

C) Está cerca de la esquina

D) Cruza la calle

Answer: B) Está a dos cuadras

16. What does "Pase el semáforo" mean?

A) Cross the street

B) Walk past the traffic light

C) Turn at the next street

D) Go straight ahead

Answer: B) Walk past the traffic light

17. If someone tells you "Gire a la izquierda," what should you do?

A) Turn right

B) Go straight

C) Turn left

D) Stop

Answer: C) Turn left

18. How do you say "Excuse me" in Spanish when asking for directions?

A) Hola

B) Gracias

C) Disculpe

D) Adiós

Answer: C) Disculpe

19. How do you say "near" in Spanish?

A) Detrás de

B) Enfrente de

C) Cerca de

D) Lejos de

Answer: C) Cerca de

20. If you want to know if a place is nearby, what would you ask?

A) ¿Está lejos?

B) ¿Está cerca?

C) ¿Es aquí?

D) ¿Está enfrente?

Answer: B) ¿Está cerca?

21. How do you ask "Is there a restaurant around here?" in Spanish?

A) ¿Cómo está el restaurante?

B) ¿Dónde está el restaurante?

C) ¿Hay un restaurante por aquí?

D) ¿Está lejos el restaurante?

Answer: C) ¿Hay un restaurante por aquí?

22. What does "Detrás de" mean?

A) In front of

B) Behind

C) Next to

D) Near

Answer: B) Behind

23. How do you confirm directions in Spanish by repeating them?

A) ¿Entonces, todo recto y luego a la derecha?

B) ¿Cuándo es todo recto?

C) ¿Dónde está la dirección?

D) ¿Qué es todo recto?

Answer: A) ¿Entonces, todo recto y luego a la derecha?

24. How do you say "square" (as in a town square) in Spanish?

A) La calle

B) La plaza

C) La avenida

D) La esquina

Answer: B) La plaza

25. What would you say if you don't know the directions?

A) No sé, lo siento.

B) Está aquí.

C) Siga todo recto.

D) Gire a la derecha.

Answer: A) No sé, lo siento.

ᗞᗞᗞ

FOUR
AT A RESTAURANT

Common Phrases

Hola, una mesa para dos, por favor. - Hello, a table for two, please.

¿Puedo ver el menú, por favor? - Can I see the menu, please?

¿Cuáles son las especialidades de la casa? - What are the house specialties?

¿Qué me recomienda? - What do you recommend?

Soy alérgico/a a... - I am allergic to...

¿Puede traerme un poco de agua, por favor? - Can you bring me some water, please?

La cuenta, por favor. - The bill, please.

Food and Drink Vocabulary

Appetizers (Entrantes)

Sopa - Soup

Ensalada - Salad

Tapas - Appetizers (small dishes)

Patatas bravas - Spicy potatoes

Main Courses (Platos principales)

Pollo - Chicken

Carne - Meat

Pescado - Fish

Vegetales - Vegetables

Pasta - Pasta

Desserts (Postres)

Tarta - Cake

Helado - Ice cream

Fruta - Fruit

Flan - Custard dessert

Drinks (Bebidas)

Agua - Water

Cerveza - Beer

Vino - Wine

Refresco - Soft drink

Café - Coffee

Ordering Food

Me gustaría pedir... - I would like to order...

Para mí, ... - For me, ...

¿Puede hacer esto sin... ? - Can you make this without...?

¿Cuánto cuesta esto? - How much does this cost?

Asking for Assistance

Disculpe, ¿puede ayudarme? - Excuse me, can you help me?

¿Dónde está el baño? - Where is the bathroom?

¿Hay opciones vegetarianas? - Are there vegetarian options?

Payment

¿Aceptan tarjetas de crédito? - Do you accept credit cards?

¿Puedo pagar por separado? - Can I pay separately?

¿Hay propina incluida? - Is the tip included?

Spanish Restaurant and Food Vocabulary Multiple-Choice Questions

1. How do you ask for a table for two in Spanish?

    A) ¿Dónde está la mesa?

B) Hola, una mesa para dos, por favor.

C) ¿Me trae la cuenta, por favor?

D) ¿Cuánto cuesta la mesa?

Answer: B) Hola, una mesa para dos, por favor.

    2. What does "¿Puedo ver el menú, por favor?" mean?

    A) Can I have the bill, please?

B) Can I see the menu, please?

C) What do you recommend?

D) What are the house specialties?

Answer: B) Can I see the menu, please?

    3. How do you ask for house specialties in Spanish?

    A) ¿Puede traerme agua, por favor?

B) ¿Cuáles son las especialidades de la casa?

C) ¿Puedo ver la cuenta, por favor?

D) ¿Aceptan tarjetas de crédito?

Answer: B) ¿Cuáles son las especialidades de la casa?

    4. If you have a food allergy, how do you say "I am allergic to..." in Spanish?

    A) ¿Puedo pedir...?

B) Soy alérgico/a a...

C) Me gustaría...

D) ¿Cuánto cuesta esto?

Answer: B) Soy alérgico/a a...

5. What does "La cuenta, por favor." mean?

A) The menu, please.

B) The bill, please.

C) A table for two, please.

D) A bottle of wine, please.

Answer: B) The bill, please.

6. What is the Spanish word for "Soup"?

A) Ensalada

B) Flan

C) Sopa

D) Tapas

Answer: C) Sopa

7. What are "Tapas" in Spanish cuisine?

A) Small dishes or appetizers

B) A type of soup

C) A dessert

D) A type of meat

Answer: A) Small dishes or appetizers

8. What does "Pescado" mean?

A) Chicken

B) Meat

C) Fish

D) Vegetables

Answer: C) Fish

9. Which of these is NOT a dessert in Spanish?

A) Helado

B) Flan

C) Tarta

D) Ensalada

Answer: D) Ensalada

10. How do you say "Water" in Spanish?

A) Refresco

B) Agua

C) Café

D) Cerveza

Answer: B) Agua

11. How do you say "Beer" in Spanish?

A) Refresco

B) Cerveza

C) Vino

D) Café

Answer: B) Cerveza

12. What is the Spanish word for "Cake"?

A) Tarta

B) Flan

C) Ensalada

D) Pasta

Answer: A) Tarta

13. What does "Me gustaría pedir..." mean?

A) I would like to order...

B) Can you bring me water?

C) What do you recommend?

D) Is the tip included?

Answer: A) I would like to order...

14. How do you say "For me, ..." in Spanish?

A) ¿Cuánto cuesta esto?

B) Para mí, ...

C) ¿Dónde está el baño?

D) Me gustaría pedir...

Answer: B) Para mí, ...

15. What does "¿Cuánto cuesta esto?" mean?

A) How much does this cost?

B) What do you recommend?

C) Can I pay separately?

D) Where is the bathroom?

Answer: A) How much does this cost?

16. How do you ask if vegetarian options are available?

A) ¿Puedo ver el menú?

B) ¿Hay opciones vegetarianas?

C) ¿Dónde está el baño?

D) ¿Aceptan tarjetas de crédito?

Answer: B) ¿Hay opciones vegetarianas?

17. How do you ask if credit cards are accepted?

A) ¿Aceptan tarjetas de crédito?

B) ¿Puedo pagar por separado?

C) ¿Dónde está el baño?

D) ¿Puede traerme un poco de agua?

Answer: A) ¿Aceptan tarjetas de crédito?

18. What does "¿Puedo pagar por separado?" mean?

A) Can I see the menu?

B) Can I pay separately?

C) Can you bring me water?

D) Do you accept credit cards?

Answer: B) Can I pay separately?

19. How do you ask if the tip is included?

A) ¿Cuáles son las especialidades de la casa?

B) ¿Dónde está el baño?

C) ¿Hay propina incluida?

D) ¿Cuánto cuesta esto?

Answer: C) ¿Hay propina incluida?

20. What does "Carne" mean in Spanish?

A) Chicken

B) Meat

C) Fish

D) Salad

Answer: B) Meat

21. How do you say "Vegetables" in Spanish?

A) Ensalada

B) Pollo

C) Vegetales

D) Tarta

Answer: C) Vegetales

22. If you need help in a restaurant, what would you say?

A) Disculpe, ¿puede ayudarme?

B) ¿Dónde está el baño?

C) ¿Cuánto cuesta esto?

D) ¿Puedo pagar con tarjeta?

Answer: A) Disculpe, ¿puede ayudarme?

23. What does "Flan" refer to in Spanish cuisine?

A) A spicy dish

B) A salad

C) A custard dessert

D) A type of bread

Answer: C) A custard dessert

24. How do you say "Wine" in Spanish?

A) Refresco

B) Cerveza

C) Agua

D) Vino

Answer: D) Vino

25. If you want to ask for something without a certain ingredient, what phrase would you use?

A) ¿Puedo pagar por separado?

B) ¿Puede hacer esto sin...?

C) ¿Dónde está el baño?

D) ¿Cuáles son las especialidades de la casa?

Answer: B) ¿Puede hacer esto sin...?

ㆆㆆㆆ

FIVE

100 Common Phrases In Spanish

Greetings and Introductions

Hola - Hello

Buenos días - Good morning

Buenas tardes - Good afternoon

Buenas noches - Good evening / Good night

¿Cómo estás? - How are you? (informal)

¿Cómo está usted? - How are you? (formal)

Estoy bien, gracias. - I'm fine, thank you.

¿Y tú? - And you? (informal)

¿Y usted? - And you? (formal)

Mucho gusto. - Nice to meet you.

Basic Questions

¿Qué tal? - How's it going?

¿Qué pasa? - What's up?

¿Cómo te llamas? - What's your name?

Me llamo... - My name is...

¿De dónde eres? - Where are you from?

Soy de... - I'm from...

¿Dónde vives? - Where do you live?

Vivo en... - I live in...

¿Hablas inglés? - Do you speak English?

¿Entiendes? - Do you understand?

Polite Expressions

Por favor - Please

Gracias - Thank you

De nada - You're welcome

Disculpe - Excuse me (formal)

Perdón - Sorry / Excuse me (informal)

Lo siento - I'm sorry

Con permiso - Excuse me (to pass by)

¿Puedes ayudarme? - Can you help me?

Claro - Of course

No hay problema - No problem

Common Phrases for Daily Life

¿Qué hora es? - What time is it?

Tengo hambre. - I'm hungry.

Tengo sed. - I'm thirsty.

Estoy cansado/cansada. - I'm tired.

¿Dónde está el baño? - Where is the bathroom?

Necesito ayuda. - I need help.

No sé. - I don't know.

No entiendo. - I don't understand.

Hace calor. - It's hot.

Hace frío. - It's cold.

Shopping and Dining

¿Cuánto cuesta? - How much does it cost?

Quiero esto. - I want this.

¿Tienes...? - Do you have...?

La cuenta, por favor. - The bill, please.

¿Qué recomiendas? - What do you recommend?

Está delicioso. - It's delicious.

Soy vegetariano/vegetariana. - I'm vegetarian.

¿Dónde está el mercado? - Where is the market?

¿Aceptan tarjetas? - Do you accept cards?

Es demasiado caro. - It's too expensive.

Travel and Directions

¿Dónde está la estación de tren? - Where is the train station?

¿Cómo llego a...? - How do I get to...?

Estoy perdido/perdida. - I'm lost.

A la derecha - To the right

A la izquierda - To the left

Todo recto - Straight ahead

¿Está lejos? - Is it far?

¿Está cerca? - Is it nearby?

¿Dónde puedo tomar un taxi? - Where can I get a taxi?

Necesito un mapa. - I need a map.

Feelings and Opinions

Estoy feliz. - I'm happy.

Estoy triste. - I'm sad.

Estoy enojado/enojada. - I'm angry.

Me gusta. - I like it.

No me gusta. - I don't like it.

Es bonito. - It's pretty.

Es feo. - It's ugly.

Es interesante. - It's interesting.

Es aburrido. - It's boring.

Estoy de acuerdo. - I agree.

At Home

¿Qué haces? - What are you doing?

Voy a cocinar. - I'm going to cook.

Voy a dormir. - I'm going to sleep.

Limpia tu cuarto. - Clean your room.

¿Qué vamos a comer? - What are we going to eat?

Apaga la luz. - Turn off the light.

Enciende la televisión. - Turn on the TV.

Estoy ocupado/ocupada. - I'm busy.

¿Puedo ayudarte? - Can I help you?

Estoy listo/lista. - I'm ready.

Work and School

Tengo que trabajar. - I have to work.

¿A qué te dedicas? - What do you do for work?

Soy estudiante. - I'm a student.

Tengo una reunión. - I have a meeting.

Estoy aprendiendo español. - I'm learning Spanish.

¿Qué estudias? - What do you study?

Tengo mucho que hacer. - I have a lot to do.

Estoy cansado/cansada de trabajar. - I'm tired of working.

¿Qué hora es tu clase? - What time is your class?

Necesito un descanso. - I need a break.

Health and Emergencies

Me siento mal. - I feel sick.

Necesito un médico. - I need a doctor.

¿Dónde está el hospital? - Where is the hospital?

Llama a una ambulancia. - Call an ambulance.

Me duele la cabeza. - My head hurts.

Tengo fiebre. - I have a fever.

¿Dónde está la farmacia? - Where is the pharmacy?

Necesito medicina. - I need medicine.

¡Ayuda! - Help!

Estoy bien. - I'm okay.

Spanish Basic Phrases and Expressions - Multiple-Choice Questions

1. How do you say "Good morning" in Spanish?

    A) Buenas noches

B) Buenos días

C) Hola

D) Buenas tardes

Answer: B) Buenos días

2. What does "¿Cómo estás?" mean?

    A) What's your name?

B) How are you? (informal)

C) Where are you from?

D) How much does it cost?

Answer: B) How are you? (informal)

3. How do you introduce yourself in Spanish?

    A) Me llamo...

B) Soy de...

C) Estoy bien...

D) Estoy cansado/cansada.

Answer: A) Me llamo...

4. How do you say "Nice to meet you" in Spanish?

    A) Gracias

B) Lo siento

C) Mucho gusto

D) Disculpe

Answer: C) Mucho gusto

5. What does "¿Qué pasa?" mean?

    A) What's up?

B) How's the weather?

C) What's your name?

D) Where do you live?

Answer: A) What's up?

6. How do you say "Please" in Spanish?

A) Gracias

B) Perdón

C) Por favor

D) Claro

Answer: C) Por favor

7. What does "De nada" mean?

A) Of course

B) You're welcome

C) No problem

D) I don't know

Answer: B) You're welcome

8. How do you say "I need help" in Spanish?

A) Tengo hambre

B) Estoy bien

C) Necesito ayuda

D) Estoy cansado/cansada

Answer: C) Necesito ayuda

9. What does "No entiendo" mean?

A) I don't understand

B) I don't know

C) I'm lost

D) I need help

Answer: A) I don't understand

10. How do you ask "Where is the bathroom?" in Spanish?

A) ¿Dónde está la estación?

B) ¿Dónde está el baño?

C) ¿Dónde está el mercado?

D) ¿Dónde está el hospital?

Answer: B) ¿Dónde está el baño?

11. What does "Hace frío" mean?

A) It's hot

B) It's cold

C) It's raining

D) It's snowing

Answer: B) It's cold

12. How do you say "I'm hungry" in Spanish?

A) Estoy cansado/cansada

B) Tengo hambre

C) Hace frío

D) Me siento mal

Answer: B) Tengo hambre

13. What does "Quiero esto" mean?

A) I want this

B) I need help

C) It's expensive

D) I like it

Answer: A) I want this

14. How do you ask "How much does it cost?" in Spanish?

A) ¿Cuánto cuesta?

B) ¿Qué hora es?

C) ¿Dónde está?

D) ¿Entiendes?

Answer: A) ¿Cuánto cuesta?

15. What does "Está delicioso" mean?

A) It's delicious

B) It's cold

C) It's ugly

D) It's spicy

Answer: A) It's delicious

16. What does "¿Dónde puedo tomar un taxi?" mean?

A) Where can I buy a ticket?

B) Where can I get a taxi?

C) How do I get there?

D) Where is the hospital?

Answer: B) Where can I get a taxi?

17. How do you say "I'm lost" in Spanish?

A) Estoy perdido/perdida

B) No sé

C) No entiendo

D) Me siento mal

Answer: A) Estoy perdido/perdida

18. What does "A la derecha" mean?

A) To the left

B) To the right

C) Straight ahead

D) At the corner

Answer: B) To the right

19. What does "Me gusta" mean?

A) I like it

B) It's delicious

C) I don't like it

D) I'm happy

Answer: A) I like it

20. How do you say "I agree" in Spanish?

A) Estoy enojado/enojada

B) Estoy de acuerdo

C) No me gusta

D) Es interesante

Answer: B) Estoy de acuerdo

21. What does "Voy a dormir" mean?

A) I'm going to cook

B) I'm going to sleep

C) I'm ready

D) I'm lost

Answer: B) I'm going to sleep

22. How do you say "Turn off the light" in Spanish?

A) Apaga la luz

B) Enciende la televisión

C) Estoy listo/lista

D) Limpia tu cuarto

Answer: A) Apaga la luz

23. What does "Soy estudiante" mean?

A) I am a student

B) I have to work

C) I need a meeting

D) I am a teacher

Answer: A) I am a student

24. How do you say "I have a meeting" in Spanish?

A) Tengo hambre

B) Tengo una reunión

C) Tengo mucho que hacer

D) Estoy cansado/cansada

Answer: B) Tengo una reunión

25. What does "Me duele la cabeza" mean?

A) My head hurts

B) I'm lost

C) I have a fever

D) I need medicine

Answer: A) My head hurts

ᐅᐅᐅ

SIX

COMMON CONVERSATIONS IN SPANISH

Greetings and Introductions

Hola - Hello

Buenos días - Good morning

Buenas tardes - Good afternoon

Buenas noches - Good evening/night

¿Cómo te llamas? - What is your name?

Me llamo... - My name is...

Mucho gusto - Nice to meet you

¿De dónde eres? - Where are you from?

Soy de... - I am from...

Asking for Directions

¿Dónde está...? - Where is...?

¿Cómo llego a...? - How do I get to...?

A la derecha - To the right

A la izquierda - To the left

Todo recto - Straight ahead

Cerca - Near

Lejos - Far

Ordering Food and Drinks

Quisiera... - I would like...

¿Qué me recomienda? - What do you recommend?

La cuenta, por favor - The bill, please

¿Está incluido el servicio? - Is the service included?

Sin gluten - Gluten-free

Vegetariano/a - Vegetarian

Shopping

¿Cuánto cuesta? - How much does it cost?

¿Puedo probarlo? - Can I try it on?

Busco... - I am looking for...

¿Tienen esto en otro color/tamaño? - Do you have this in another color/size?

Es demasiado caro - It's too expensive

Making Small Talk

¿Cómo estás? - How are you?

Estoy bien, gracias - I am fine, thank you

¿Qué tal tu día? - How is your day?

Hace buen tiempo hoy - It's nice weather today

¿Tienes planes para el fin de semana? - Do you have plans for the weekend?

Expressing Opinions

Me gusta - I like it

No me gusta - I don't like it

Es interesante - It's interesting

Creo que... - I think that...

Es una buena idea - It's a good idea

Common Conversations

1. Greetings and Introductions

A: Hola, ¿cómo estás?
B: Hola, estoy bien, gracias. ¿Y tú?
A: Estoy bien también. ¿Cómo te llamas?
B: Me llamo Ana. ¿Y tú?

A: Me llamo Carlos. Mucho gusto.
B: Mucho gusto.

Translation:
A: Hi, how are you?
B: Hi, I'm fine, thank you. And you?
A: I'm fine too. What's your name?
B: My name is Ana. And you?
A: My name is Carlos. Nice to meet you.
B: Nice to meet you.

2. Asking for Directions

A: Disculpe, ¿dónde está el banco?
B: Está a dos cuadras. Siga todo recto y gire a la derecha en la esquina.
A: ¿Está lejos?

B: No, está a cinco minutos caminando.
A: Muchas gracias.
B: De nada.

Translation:
A: Excuse me, where is the bank?
B: It's two blocks away. Go straight and turn right at the corner.
A: Is it far?
B: No, it's a five-minute walk.
A: Thank you very much.
B: You're welcome.

3. At a Restaurant

A: Buenas tardes, una mesa para dos, por favor.
B: Claro, síganme.
A: Gracias. ¿Qué recomienda?

B: *El plato del día es muy bueno.*
A: *Perfecto, lo tomaremos.*
B: *¿Algo más?*
A: *Sí, una botella de agua, por favor.*

Translation:
A: *Good afternoon, a table for two, please.*
B: *Of course, follow me.*
A: *Thank you. What do you recommend?*
B: *The daily special is very good.*
A: *Perfect, we'll take that.*
B: *Anything else?*
A: *Yes, a bottle of water, please.*

4. Shopping

A: Hola, ¿cuánto cuesta esta camisa?
B: Cuesta 20 euros.
A: ¿Tiene una talla más grande?
B: Sí, aquí tiene.
A: Me la llevo. ¿Aceptan tarjetas?
B: Sí, aceptamos tarjetas.

Translation:
A: Hi, how much does this shirt cost?
B: It costs 20 euros.
A: Do you have a larger size?
B: Yes, here you go.
A: I'll take it. Do you accept cards?
B: Yes, we accept cards.

5. At the Hotel

A: *Hola, tengo una reserva a nombre de García.*
B: *Sí, aquí está. ¿Para cuántas noches?*
A: *Para tres noches.*
B: *Perfecto. Aquí tiene su llave. El desayuno es de 7 a 10 en el primer piso.*
A: *Gracias. ¿Hay Wi-Fi?*
B: *Sí, la contraseña está en la tarjeta.*

Translation:
A: *Hi, I have a reservation under the name García.*
B: *Yes, here it is. For how many nights?*
A: *For three nights.*
B: *Perfect. Here is your key. Breakfast is from 7 to 10 on the first floor.*
A: *Thank you. Is there Wi-Fi?*
B: *Yes, the password is on the card.*

6. At the Airport

A: ¿Dónde está la puerta de embarque 12?
B: Está al final del pasillo, a la izquierda.
A: ¿A qué hora sale el vuelo?
B: Sale a las 3 de la tarde.
A: Gracias.
B: De nada.

Translation:
A: Where is gate 12?
B: It's at the end of the hallway, on the left.
A: What time does the flight leave?
B: It leaves at 3 p.m.
A: Thank you.
B: You're welcome.

7. Talking About the Weather

A: *Hace mucho calor hoy, ¿no?*
B: *Sí, demasiado. Prefiero el frío.*
A: *Yo también. ¿Qué tiempo hará mañana?*
B: *Según el pronóstico, va a llover.*
A: *Oh, qué mal.*

Translation:
A: *It's very hot today, isn't it?*
B: *Yes, too hot. I prefer the cold.*
A: *Me too. What will the weather be like tomorrow?*
B: *According to the forecast, it's going to rain.*
A: *Oh, that's too bad.*

8. Making Plans

A: *¿Qué haces este fin de semana?*
B: *No tengo planes. ¿Por qué?*
A: *Vamos al cine. ¿Quieres venir?*

B: ¡Claro! ¿A qué hora?
A: A las 7 de la tarde.
B: Perfecto, nos vemos allí.

Translation:
A: What are you doing this weekend?
B: I don't have plans. Why?
A: We're going to the movies. Do you want to come?
B: Of course! What time?
A: At 7 p.m.
B: Perfect, see you there.

Spanish Conversations & Vocabulary - Multiple-Choice Questions

1. What is the correct translation of "Good evening" in Spanish?

    A) Buenos días

B) Buenas noches

C) Buenas tardes

D) Hola

Answer: B) Buenas noches

    2. How do you say "My name is..." in Spanish?

    A) Soy de...

B) Me llamo...

C) ¿Cómo estás?

D) Mucho gusto

Answer: B) Me llamo...

    3. What does "¿De dónde eres?" mean?

    A) Where are you from?

B) What is your name?

C) How are you?

D) Where do you live?

Answer: A) Where are you from?

    4. How do you ask for directions in Spanish?

A) ¿Dónde está...?

B) ¿Cómo te llamas?

C) ¿A qué te dedicas?

D) Me gusta

Answer: A) ¿Dónde está...?

5. What does "A la derecha" mean?

A) To the left

B) To the right

C) Straight ahead

D) Near

Answer: B) To the right

6. How do you say "Far" in Spanish?

A) Cerca

B) Lejos

C) A la izquierda

D) Todo recto

Answer: B) Lejos

7. What does "La cuenta, por favor" mean?

A) The bill, please

B) A table for two, please

C) The food is delicious

D) What do you recommend?

Answer: A) The bill, please

8. How do you say "I would like..." in Spanish when ordering food?

A) ¿Cuánto cuesta?

B) Quisiera...

C) Es demasiado caro

D) Me gusta

Answer: B) Quisiera...

9. If you want to ask if service is included in a restaurant, you say:

A) ¿Aceptan tarjetas?

B) ¿Está incluido el servicio?

C) ¿Dónde está el baño?

D) ¿Tienes esto en otro color?

Answer: B) ¿Está incluido el servicio?

10. How do you ask for the price of an item in Spanish?

A) ¿Puedo probarlo?

B) ¿Tienen esto en otro color?

C) ¿Cuánto cuesta?

D) Busco...

Answer: C) ¿Cuánto cuesta?

11. What does "Es demasiado caro" mean?

A) It's too expensive

B) It's delicious

C) I like it

D) I don't understand

Answer: A) It's too expensive

12. How do you ask "Do you have this in another size?" in Spanish?

A) ¿Dónde está el mercado?

B) ¿Aceptan tarjetas?

C) ¿Tienen esto en otro tamaño?

D) Me gusta

Answer: C) ¿Tienen esto en otro tamaño?

13. How do you say "What do you recommend?" in Spanish?

A) ¿Dónde está la estación?

B) ¿Qué me recomienda?

C) ¿A qué hora sale el vuelo?

D) ¿Dónde está la puerta de embarque?

Answer: B) ¿Qué me recomienda?

14. What does "Hace buen tiempo hoy" mean?

A) It's raining today

B) It's nice weather today

C) It's too cold today

D) It's very windy today

Answer: B) It's nice weather today

15. How do you say "I think that..." in Spanish?

A) Creo que...

B) Me gusta...

C) No me gusta...

D) Estoy de acuerdo

Answer: A) Creo que...

16. If someone asks "¿Qué tal tu día?" what are they asking?

A) How is your day?

B) How are you?

C) Where do you live?

D) Do you like this?

Answer: A) How is your day?

17. What does "Voy a dormir" mean?

A) I'm going to sleep

B) I'm going to eat

C) I'm going to buy

D) I'm going to run

Answer: A) I'm going to sleep

18. If you want to book a hotel room, how would you say "I have a reservation under the name García"?

A) ¿Cuánto cuesta la habitación?

B) Hola, tengo una reserva a nombre de García.

C) ¿Dónde está la recepción?

D) ¿A qué hora es el desayuno?

Answer: B) Hola, tengo una reserva a nombre de García.

19. What does "El desayuno es de 7 a 10 en el primer piso" mean?

A) The hotel has free Wi-Fi

B) The breakfast is from 7 to 10 on the first floor

C) The room service is available 24/7

D) The dinner is included in the price

Answer: B) The breakfast is from 7 to 10 on the first floor

20. How do you ask "Where is gate 12?" at the airport?

A) ¿Dónde está la puerta de embarque 12?

B) ¿Dónde está la estación de tren?

C) ¿Dónde puedo tomar un taxi?

D) ¿Qué tiempo hará mañana?

Answer: A) ¿Dónde está la puerta de embarque 12?

21. If someone says "Prefiero el frío," what are they saying?

A) I prefer the heat

B) I prefer the cold

C) I prefer the rain

D) I prefer the summer

Answer: B) I prefer the cold

    22. What does "Vamos al cine. ¿Quieres venir?" mean?

    A) We're going to the park. Do you want to come?

B) We're going to the cinema. Do you want to come?

C) We're going to the restaurant. Do you want to come?

D) We're going to the shopping mall. Do you want to come?

Answer: B) We're going to the cinema. Do you want to come?

    23. How do you say "See you there" in Spanish?

    A) Nos vemos allí

B) Hasta luego

C) Nos vemos pronto

D) Adiós

Answer: A) Nos vemos allí

    24. What does "¿Tienes planes para el fin de semana?" mean?

    A) Do you have a meeting this weekend?

B) Do you have plans for the weekend?

C) What's the weather like this weekend?

D) Are you working this weekend?

Answer: B) Do you have plans for the weekend?

    25. How do you ask "What time does the flight leave?" in Spanish?

    A) ¿Dónde está el aeropuerto?

B) ¿A qué hora sale el vuelo?

C) ¿Dónde está la maleta?

D) ¿A qué hora es el desayuno?

Answer: B) ¿A qué hora sale el vuelo?

ppp

SEVEN
100 Commonly Used Sentences

English Version/ Spanish Version

Hello.
Hola.

How are you?
¿Cómo estás?

What is your name?
¿Cuál es tu nombre?

My name is...
Me llamo...

Nice to meet you.
Mucho gusto.

Please.
Por favor.

Thank you.
Gracias.

You're welcome.
De nada.

Excuse me.
Disculpe.

I'm sorry.
Lo siento.

Yes.
Sí.

No.
No.

Maybe.
Tal vez.

I don't understand.
No entiendo.

Can you help me?
¿Puedes ayudarme?

Where is the bathroom?
¿Dónde está el baño?

How much does this cost?
¿Cuánto cuesta esto?

I would like...
Me gustaría...

What time is it?
¿Qué hora es?

I am hungry.
Tengo hambre.

I am thirsty.
Tengo sed.

I am tired.
Estoy cansado/a.

I love you.
Te amo.

What do you do?
¿A qué te dedicas?

I work as a...
Trabajo como...

Where are you from?
¿De dónde eres?

I am from...
Soy de...

Do you speak English?
¿Hablas inglés?

I speak a little Spanish.
Hablo un poco de español.

Can you repeat that?
¿Puedes repetir eso?

I need a doctor.
Necesito un médico.

Call the police!
¡Llama a la policía!

I am lost.
Estoy perdido/a.

Can you show me?
¿Puedes mostrarme?

I like this.
Me gusta esto.

I don't like this.
No me gusta esto.

It is beautiful.
Es hermoso/a.

It is hot today.
Hace calor hoy.

It is cold today.
Hace frío hoy.

What is your favorite food?
¿Cuál es tu comida favorita?

I am learning Spanish.
Estoy aprendiendo español.

What do you recommend?
¿Qué recomiendas?

I need to go.
Necesito irme.

See you later.
Hasta luego.

Have a good day.
Que tengas un buen día.

Good night.
Buenas noches.

I am happy.
Estoy feliz.

I am sad.
Estoy triste.

I am excited.
Estoy emocionado/a.

I am bored.
Estoy aburrido/a.

What are you doing?
¿Qué estás haciendo?

I am watching TV.
Estoy viendo la televisión.

I am reading a book.
Estoy leyendo un libro.

I like to travel.
Me gusta viajar.

I want to go home.
Quiero ir a casa.

I need to study.
Necesito estudiar.

What is your phone number?
¿Cuál es tu número de teléfono?

Can I borrow this?
¿Puedo tomar prestado esto?

I am on my way.
Estoy en camino.

I will be there soon.
Estaré allí pronto.

What is the weather like?
¿Cómo está el clima?

It is raining.
Está lloviendo.

It is sunny.
Está soleado.

I am going to the store.
Voy a la tienda.

Do you want to join me?
¿Quieres acompañarme?

I have a question.
Tengo una pregunta.

Can you explain that?
¿Puedes explicar eso?

I am ready.
Estoy listo/a.

I am not sure.
No estoy seguro/a.

Let's go!
¡Vamos!

I need to relax.
Necesito relajarme.

I feel sick.
Me siento enfermo/a.

I am looking for...
Estoy buscando...

Can you recommend a restaurant?
¿Puedes recomendar un restaurante?

I would like to make a reservation.
Me gustaría hacer una reserva.

What is your favorite color?
¿Cuál es tu color favorito?

I enjoy listening to music.
Disfruto escuchar música.

I like to cook.
Me gusta cocinar.

I am going to bed.
Me voy a la cama.

I need some rest.
Necesito descansar.

What do you think?
¿Qué piensas?

I agree.
Estoy de acuerdo.

I disagree.
No estoy de acuerdo.

That sounds good.
Suena bien.

I am proud of you.
Estoy orgulloso/a de ti.

I appreciate your help.
Aprecio tu ayuda.

I am grateful.
Estoy agradecido/a.

I hope you have a great time.
Espero que lo pases bien.

I will miss you.
Te voy a extrañar.

Let's keep in touch.
Mantengámonos en contacto.

I am excited for the weekend.
Estoy emocionado/a por el fin de semana.

I have to go now.
Tengo que irme ahora.

I will call you later.
Te llamaré más tarde.

I am looking forward to it.
Estoy deseando que llegue.

I had a great time.
Pasé un gran momento.

I hope to see you soon.
Espero verte pronto.

Take care!
¡Cuídate!

Safe travels!
¡Buen viaje!

Enjoy your meal!
¡Buen provecho!

Goodbye!
¡Adiós!

Multiple Type Questions

1. How do you say "Hello" in Spanish?

a) Gracias

b) Hola

c) Adiós

d) Por favor

Answer: b) Hola

2. What is the Spanish word for "Thank you"?

a) Disculpe

b) Lo siento

c) Gracias

d) De nada

Answer: c) Gracias

3. How do you say "Excuse me" in Spanish?

a) Lo siento

b) De nada

c) Disculpe

d) Gracias

Answer: c) Disculpe

4. What does "Buenas noches" mean?

a) Good morning

b) Good afternoon

c) Good night

d) Good day

Answer: c) Good night

5. What is the Spanish translation for "I am hungry"?

a) Estoy cansado/a

b) Tengo hambre

c) Estoy perdido/a

d) Tengo sed

Answer: b) Tengo hambre

6. How do you ask "Where is the bathroom?" in Spanish?

a) ¿Dónde está el baño?

b) ¿Dónde está la tienda?

c) ¿Dónde está el hospital?

d) ¿Dónde está el banco?

Answer: a) ¿Dónde está el baño?

7. What does "Estoy perdido/a" mean in English?

a) I am lost

b) I am tired

c) I am happy

d) I am thirsty

Answer: a) I am lost

8. What is the Spanish phrase for "I need a doctor"?

a) Necesito un médico

b) Necesito un banco

c) Necesito un coche

d) Necesito un hotel

Answer: a) Necesito un médico

9. How do you say "Can you help me?" in Spanish?

a) ¿Puedes ayudarme?

b) ¿Puedes llamarme?

c) ¿Puedes esperarme?

d) ¿Puedes seguirme?

Answer: a) ¿Puedes ayudarme?

10. Which of the following means "I love you" in Spanish?

a) Te amo

b) Te odio

c) Te espero

d) Te escucho

Answer: a) Te amo

11. What is the translation for "I like this"?

a) No me gusta esto

b) Me gusta esto

c) Me gustaría esto

d) Estoy buscando esto

Answer: b) Me gusta esto

12. How do you say "I am tired" in Spanish?

a) Estoy emocionado/a

b) Estoy cansado/a

c) Estoy triste

d) Estoy feliz

Answer: b) Estoy cansado/a

13. What does "Hace calor hoy" mean?

a) It is hot today

b) It is raining today

c) It is cold today

d) It is sunny today

Answer: a) It is hot today

14. Which phrase means "Call the police!" in Spanish?

a) ¡Llama al hospital!

b) ¡Llama a la policía!

c) ¡Llama a la tienda!

d) ¡Llama al hotel!

Answer: b) ¡Llama a la policía!

15. What is the Spanish phrase for "I am learning Spanish"?

a) Estoy aprendiendo inglés

b) Estoy aprendiendo francés

c) Estoy aprendiendo español

d) Estoy aprendiendo alemán

Answer: c) Estoy aprendiendo español

16. How do you say "I need to go" in Spanish?

a) Necesito dormir

b) Necesito comer

c) Necesito irme

d) Necesito estudiar

Answer: c) Necesito irme

17. What is the Spanish equivalent of "What is your favorite food?"

a) ¿Cuál es tu comida favorita?

b) ¿Cuál es tu color favorito?

c) ¿Cuál es tu bebida favorita?

d) ¿Cuál es tu película favorita?

Answer: a) ¿Cuál es tu comida favorita?

18. Which of these means "Can you repeat that?" in Spanish?

a) ¿Puedes recomendar un restaurante?

b) ¿Puedes mostrarme?

c) ¿Puedes repetir eso?

d) ¿Puedes acompañarme?

Answer: c) ¿Puedes repetir eso?

19. What is the translation for "See you later"?

a) Hasta luego

b) Adiós

c) Te extraño

d) Te amo

Answer: a) Hasta luego

20. How do you say "Safe travels" in Spanish?

a) ¡Buen día!

b) ¡Buen provecho!

c) ¡Buen viaje!

d) ¡Buena suerte!

Answer: c) ¡Buen viaje!

21. What does "Estoy emocionado/a" mean?

a) I am sad

b) I am excited

c) I am sick

d) I am hungry

Answer: b) I am excited

22. What is the Spanish word for "Maybe"?

a) Siempre

b) Nunca

c) Tal vez

d) Seguro

Answer: c) Tal vez

23. How do you say "It is raining" in Spanish?

a) Está soleado

b) Está lloviendo

c) Está nevando

d) Está frío

Answer: b) Está lloviendo

24. What does "Voy a la tienda" mean?

a) I am going to the school

b) I am going to the store

c) I am going to the bank

d) I am going to the hospital

Answer: b) I am going to the store

25. How do you say "I hope to see you soon" in Spanish?

a) Espero verte pronto

b) Te extraño

c) Hasta luego

d) Nos vemos después

Answer: a) Espero verte pronto

ᗭᗭᗭ

Books By The Same Author

Scan Here
FOR QUALITY BOOKS
For Home Library for
Parents, Educators &Students

www.ingramcontent.com/pod-product-compliance
Lightning Source LLC
Chambersburg PA
CBHW040907130726
48005CB00019BA/3003